Fort Necessity National Battlefield and Friendship Hill National Historic Site
Weather of 2009

Natural Resource Data Series NPS/ERMN/NRDS—2010/084

Paul Knight, Tiffany Wisniewski, Chad Bahrmann, and Sonya Miller

Pennsylvania State Climate Office
503 Walker Building
Pennsylvania State University
University Park, Pennsylvania

September 2010

U.S. Department of the Interior
National Park Service
Natural Resource Program Center
Fort Collins, Colorado

The National Park Service, Natural Resource Program Center publishes a range of reports that address natural resource topics of interest and applicability to a broad audience in the National Park Service and others in natural resource management, including scientists, conservation and environmental constituencies, and the public.

The Natural Resource Data Series is intended for timely release of basic data sets and data summaries. Care has been taken to assure accuracy of raw data values, but a thorough analysis and interpretation of the data has not been completed. Consequently, the initial analyses of data in this report are provisional and subject to change.

All manuscripts in the series receive the appropriate level of peer review to ensure that the information is scientifically credible, technically accurate, appropriately written for the intended audience, and designed and published in a professional manner. This report received informal peer review by subject-matter experts who were not directly involved in the collection, analysis, or reporting of the data. Data in this report were collected and analyzed using methods based on established, peer-reviewed protocols and were analyzed and interpreted within the guidelines of the protocols.

Views, statements, findings, conclusions, recommendations, and data in this report do not necessarily reflect views and policies of the National Park Service, U.S. Department of the Interior. Mention of trade names or commercial products does not constitute endorsement or recommendation for use by the U.S. Government.

This report is available from Eastern Rivers and Mountains Network (http://science.nature.nps.gov/im/units/ERMN) and the Natural Resource Publications Management website (http://www.nature.nps.gov/publications/NRPM).

Please cite this publication as:

Knight, P., T. Wisniewski, C. Bahrmann, and S. Miller. 2010. Fort Necessity National Battlefield and Friendship Hill National Historic Site: Weather of 2009. Natural Resource Data Series NPS/ERMN/NRDS—2010/084. National Park Service, Fort Collins, Colorado.

NPS 336/105525, 476/105525, September 2010

Table of Contents

Figures

Tables

List of Key Acronyms

COOP   National Weather Service Cooperative Observer Program

CWOP   Citizen Weather Observer Program

ERMN   Eastern Rivers and Mountains Network

FAA   Federal Aviation Administration

FONE   Fort Necessity National Battlefield

FRHI   Friendship Hill National Historic Site

GOES   Geostationary Operational Environmental Satellite

IFLOWS   Integrated Flood Observing and Warning System

NADP   National Atmospheric Deposition Program

NARR   North American Regional Reanalysis

NB   National Battlefield

NCDC   National Climatic Data Center

NHS   National Historic Site

NOAA   National Oceanic and Atmospheric Administration

NWS   National Weather Service

PDSI   Palmer Drought Severity Index

POR   Period of Record

PRISM   Parameter-elevation Regressions on Independent Slopes Model

RAWS   Remote Automated Weather Stations

USDM   United States Drought Monitor

USGS   United States Geological Survey

Introduction

Weather and climate are widely recognized as key drivers of terrestrial and aquatic ecosystems, affecting biotic as well as abiotic ecosystem characteristics and processes. Global and regional scale climatic patterns, trends, and variations are critical to the cycling of elements, nutrients, and minerals through the ecosystems and can deliver pollutants from regional and even global sources (National Assessment Synthesis Team 2001). These variations and trends influence the fundamental properties of ecologic systems such as soil-water relationships and plant-soil processes and their disturbance rates and intensity. Information obtained from meteorological monitoring will be useful to interpreting and understanding changes in species composition, community structure, water and soil chemistry, and related landscape processes (Marshall and Piekielek 2007).

The purpose of this report is to provide a concise weather and climate summary for January 1 to December 31, 2009, and to place current patterns and trends in an appropriate historical and regional context (Knight et al., in preparation). It is our intention that this report will satisfy an inherent interest in meteorological phenomena and meet portions of the Eastern Rivers and Mountains Network (ERMN) Weather and Climate Monitoring objectives:

- Document long-term trends in weather and climate through seasonal and annual summaries of selected parameters (e.g., multiple forms of precipitation, temperature).
- Identify and document extremes and averages of climatic conditions for common parameters (e.g., precipitation, air temperature) and other parameters where sufficient data are available (e.g., wind speed and direction, solar radiation).
- Provide information on near real-time weather parameters, historical climate patterns, and climate station metadata from a single, easy-to-use Internet portal.

To accomplish these objectives, a variety of atmospheric data streams were evaluated for their quality, longevity, and applicability to the ERMN parks. Since no single weather-observing network contains all the pertinent measures of atmospheric phenomena to assess ecosystem health, an objective analysis of the data networks was developed and outlined in the Weather and Climate Monitoring Protocol for the Eastern Rivers and Mountains Network and Mid-Atlantic Network of the National Park Service (Knight et al., in preparation). Through this analysis, a select number of weather/climate-observing stations were chosen as representative of each park; these are the primary data sources used to profile climate summary and trends.

In addition to a suite of summary tables, graphs, and narratives, we specifically identify a series of key climatological indicators to report status and trends on an annual basis and periodically in separate and more thorough reports. These key indicators are further described in the protocol (Knight et al., in preparation) and summarized in the body of this report.

The Climate of the Southwest Plateau

Fort Necessity National Battlefield (NB) and Friendship Hill National Historic Site (NHS) are located in Pennsylvania Climate Division 9, the "Southwest Plateau." A climate division is a region that is reasonably homogenous with respect to climatic and hydrologic characteristics and is frequently used for compiling climate statistics (http://www.esrl.noaa.gov/psd/data/usclimate/map.html). Pennsylvania is divided into 10 climate divisions.

The Southwest Plateau is generally considered to have a humid, continental type of climate, but the elevated terrain and rolling hills keep temperatures a bit lower than surrounding areas. The prevailing westerly winds carry most of the weather disturbances that affect the region from the interior of the continent, with the Atlantic Ocean having only occasional influence on the climate of the area (Davey et al., 2006). Coastal storms do, at times, affect the day-to-day weather, especially in winter, though the air circulating southeastward from the Great Lakes dominates in the winter. Seldom do storms of tropical origin have a direct effect in this part of Pennsylvania, but the rough terrain has led to memorable floods in the warm half of the year (Gelber 2002).

Temperatures are moderately continental, with the tempering effects of the Great Lakes contributing to cloud production in the winter and mountain-valley circulation-induced clouds reducing the heat during the summer. The lowest readings in the winter occur with polar air masses of Canadian origin settling over the Northeast after a fresh snowfall. The highest readings of summer happen when the sub-tropical fair weather system, the Bermuda high, pushes westward into the Carolinas; its clockwise circulation will direct hot, humid air from the Gulf region into the Laurel Highlands. Annual maximum and minimum temperatures tend to be greater in Friendship Hill NHS than in Fort Necessity NB. The average annual maximum temperature in Chalk Hill, PA, is 54.4°F (12.4°C), while the annual maximum temperature in Grays Woods, PA, is 63.4°F (17.4°C). The last freeze in the region typically occurs in early May and the first frosts appear in late September or October.

Precipitation is fairly evenly distributed throughout the year. Annual amounts generally range between 36–54 in (914–1,372 mm), while the majority of places receive 40–46 in (1,016–1,372 mm). Greatest amounts usually occur in the spring and summer months, while February is the driest month, having about 2.0 in (51 mm) less than the wettest months. Precipitation tends to be somewhat greater in the higher terrain due to uplift and additional moisture from the Great Lakes. Annual snowfall amounts are much greater for Fort Necessity NB than Friendship Hill NHS.

Surface winds blow from the west and northwest in the cold season and from the southwest during the warm half of the year. Thunderstorms follow a frequency that matches the solar cycle between the equinoxes and reaches a peak near the summer solstice. Hail is relatively infrequent, but flash floods and damaging thunderstorm winds affect parts of the region each summer. On average, tornadoes pass through the area about once every two years. Ice storms, which can cause significant disruption, occur at irregular intervals and are primarily confined to the months between December and March (Kocin and Uccellini 2004).

Observing Stations

A total of nine weather observing stations comprised of five observing networks were selected around Fort Necessity NB and Friendship Hill NHS. Representative stations within a 100-km range of each park were chosen based on several criteria, which include proximity to the park, the representativeness of the station to the park elevation profile, the type and frequency of observations, the period of record of the data, and data availability (Knight et al., in preparation). A subset of these observing networks (CASTNET, IFLOWS and GOES; three total stations) are not yet utilized for these reports due to limited data availability and/or lack of data quality assurance (Bureau of Land Management 1997). Moreover, the percentage of time a station reports particular parameters (e.g., temperature) can influence data inclusion. No stations were excluded in 2009 based on this criterion; therefore, a total of six stations were used for this report (Figure 1, Table 1).

In addition to the summary information available in this report, a near real-time data stream has been made available to the ERMN through a Web interface for the selected stations, along with monthly, seasonal, and annual summaries. The Web interface is accessible through the following link: http://climate.met.psu.edu/gmaps/NPS_DEVELOPMENT/interface.php.

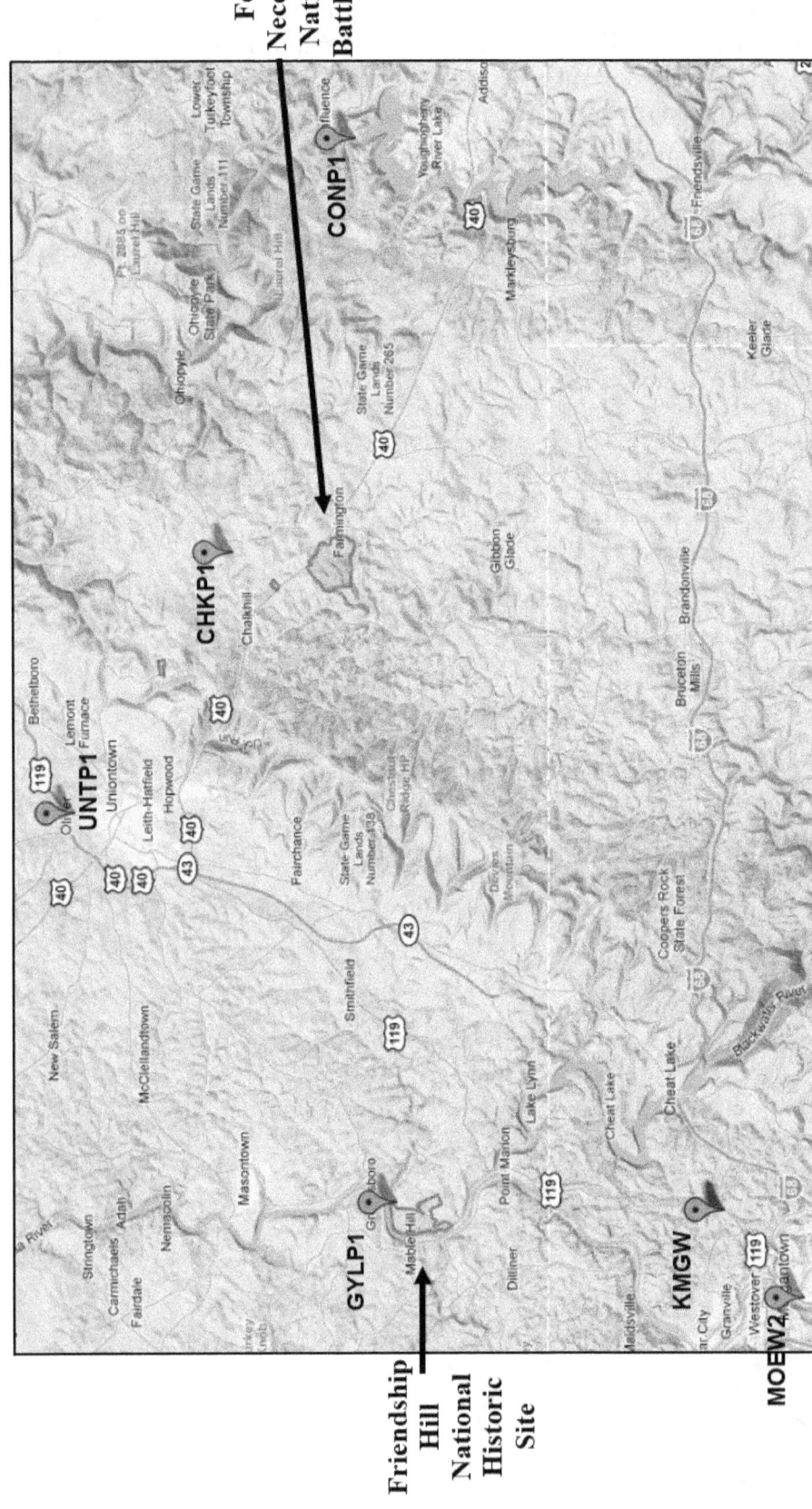

Figure 1. Location of weather observing stations around Friendship Hill NHS and Fort Necessity NB.

Table 1. List of weather observing stations around Friendship Hill NHS and Fort Necessity NB selected as best representative of the parks in 2009.

Station	Observing Network	Station Name	Period of Record (POR)		Percentage of Time Reporting Temperature for 2009	Percentage of Time Reporting Precipitation for 2009	Percentage of Time Reporting Temperature for entire POR	Percentage of Time Reporting Precipitation for entire POR
CHKP1	COOP	Chalk Hill 2 ENE	07/01/1977	Present	100.0	98.6	99.9	99.9
GYLP1	COOP	Grays Landing	10/01/1996	Present	100.0	100.0	94.2	98.3
UNTP1	COOP	Uniontown 1 NE	01/01/1894	Present	100.0	99.5	97.3	95.6
CONP1	COOP	Confluence	07/01/1946	Present	100.0	99.5	99.7	99.7
MOEW2	COOP	Morgantown Lock and Dam	09/01/1921	Present	99.7	99.7	97.4*	96.1
KMGW	FAA	Morgantown Airport	12/31/1973	Present	100.0	100.0	99.0	99.0

* Percentage of time reporting temperature for Morgantown Lock and Dam is based upon a period of record beginning on 06/01/1944. This station did not report temperature prior to this date.

Temperature Summary

In calendar year 2009 temperatures averaged lower than normal (Table 2), primarily due to a cold January and December, as well as a chilly June, July, and October (Figures 2 and 3). The maps in Figures 2 and 3 were created using estimates from the Parameter-elevation Regressions on Independent Slopes Model (PRISM). PRISM uses an interpolation scheme for temperature between actual observations and corrects these estimates for changes in topography across the region (Daly et al. 2002). More information can be found at http://www.prism.oregonstate.edu/.

The year began quite cold as January had readings ranging from -3.5 degrees Fahrenheit (°F) (-1.9 degrees Celsius (°C)) to -6.6°F (-3.7°C) below normal (Tables 3 and 4). The coldest weather of the year occurred on January 17–18 when minima of -23°F (-29°C) were measured at Chalk Hill, PA and a value of -4°F (-20°C) occurred at Morgantown Lock and Dam (Table 2). February temperatures returned to average with a +0.4°F (+0.2°C) temperature anomaly in Confluence, PA, a site near Fort Necessity NB (Table 4). Very chilly nighttime air returned late in the month and early in March with the readings -2°F (-19°C) on February 25 and +2°F (-17°C) on March 5 at Chalk Hill. The first month with well above average temperatures was March which ranked as the 36th warmest on record since 1895 (Figures 2 and 3). Overall, the winter was the 45th chilliest on record (Table 5).

The spring ranked the 47th coolest on record since 1895 which is very close to normal (Table 5). Two of the spring months had below average temperatures for the majority of the reporting stations (Table 4). The largest anomalies were in June at Chalk Hill which tallied an anomaly of -3.1°F (-1.7°C), mainly due to abundant cloud suppressing daytime readings (Table 4). Nighttime temperatures were very close to the long-term average (Figure 3). The last freeze of the season occurred on May 20th, though scattered frost was noted as late as June 1st in some areas. There were five consecutive days with readings in the 80's°F (> 27°C) from April 25–29.

Summer of 2009 was much cooler than normal, ranking as the 11th chilliest on record (Table 5). This negative anomaly was due, in large part, to the coldest July in 115 years, nearly 0.5°F (0.3°C) lower than the previous record (1984) (Figures 2 and 3). The other two months consisted of nearly normal temperatures with August slightly warmer than usual and September just a bit cooler than normal (Table 4). The highest temperature of the summer occurred during August with a reading of 85.0°F (29.4°C) on the 18th. However, the highest reading of 2009 occurred in late April with a reading of 86°F (30.2°C) at Chalk Hill on the 28th (Table 2). Morning readings in early September dropped to 38°F (3.3°C) on the 2nd, but the first frost did not come for another month.

Temperatures in autumn were nearly normal, ranking 52nd coolest since records have been kept in 1895 (Table 5). The first 32°F (0°C) reading of the fall occurred on October 6th near Fort Necessity NB, leading to a shorter than normal length of the growing season (Table 2). November was the 8th warmest since 1895 and the mildest since 2003. December was below normal (Figures 2 and 3) with a temperature ranking of 34th coolest. Readings dropped to or below 0°F (-17.9°C) twice during late December. There were more than the average number of cold days and near to above average number of cold nights (Table 2). The growing season length ranged between 139 and 189 days, close to the long-term average (Table 2).

Table 2. Status of 2009 temperature indicators compared to the 30-year normal (1971–2000) at the Chalk Hill (CHKP1) and Morgantown Lock and Dam (MOEW2) stations.

Temperature Indicator	CHKP1 2009	CHKP1 1971–2000	MOEW2 2009	MOEW2 1971–2000
Average Annual Temperature	45.9°F 7.7°C	48.4°F 9.1°C	51.3°F 10.7°C	52.9°F 11.6°C
Average Annual Maximum Temperature	56.6°F 13.7°C	58.5°F 14.7°C	61.6°F 16.4	63.5°F 17.5°C
Summer Maximum (highest temperature)	86.0°F 30.0°C	87.3°F 30.7°C	90.0°F 32.2°C	93.3°F 34.1°C
Hot Days (days with Tmax≥90°F/32°C)	0	1	1	8
Average Annual Minimum Temperature	35.2°F 1.8°C	39.2°F 4.0°C	41.1°F 5.1°C	41.8°F 5.4°C
Winter Minimum (lowest temperature)	-23.0°F -30.6°C	-11.0°F -23.9°C	-4.0°F -20.0°C	-4.4°F -20.2
Cold Days (days with Tmax≤32°F/0°F)	50	40	32	22
Sub-freezing Nights (days with Tmin≤32°F/0°C)	152	133	116	116
Cold Winter Nights (days with Tmin≤0°F/-17.8°C)	10	7	3	3
Growing Season Length (days between last spring 32°F/0°C and first fall 32°F/0°C)	139	145	189	172

Friendship Hill NHS and Fort Necessity NB
Departure from Average Monthly Maximum Temperature
2009 vs. 1971–2000

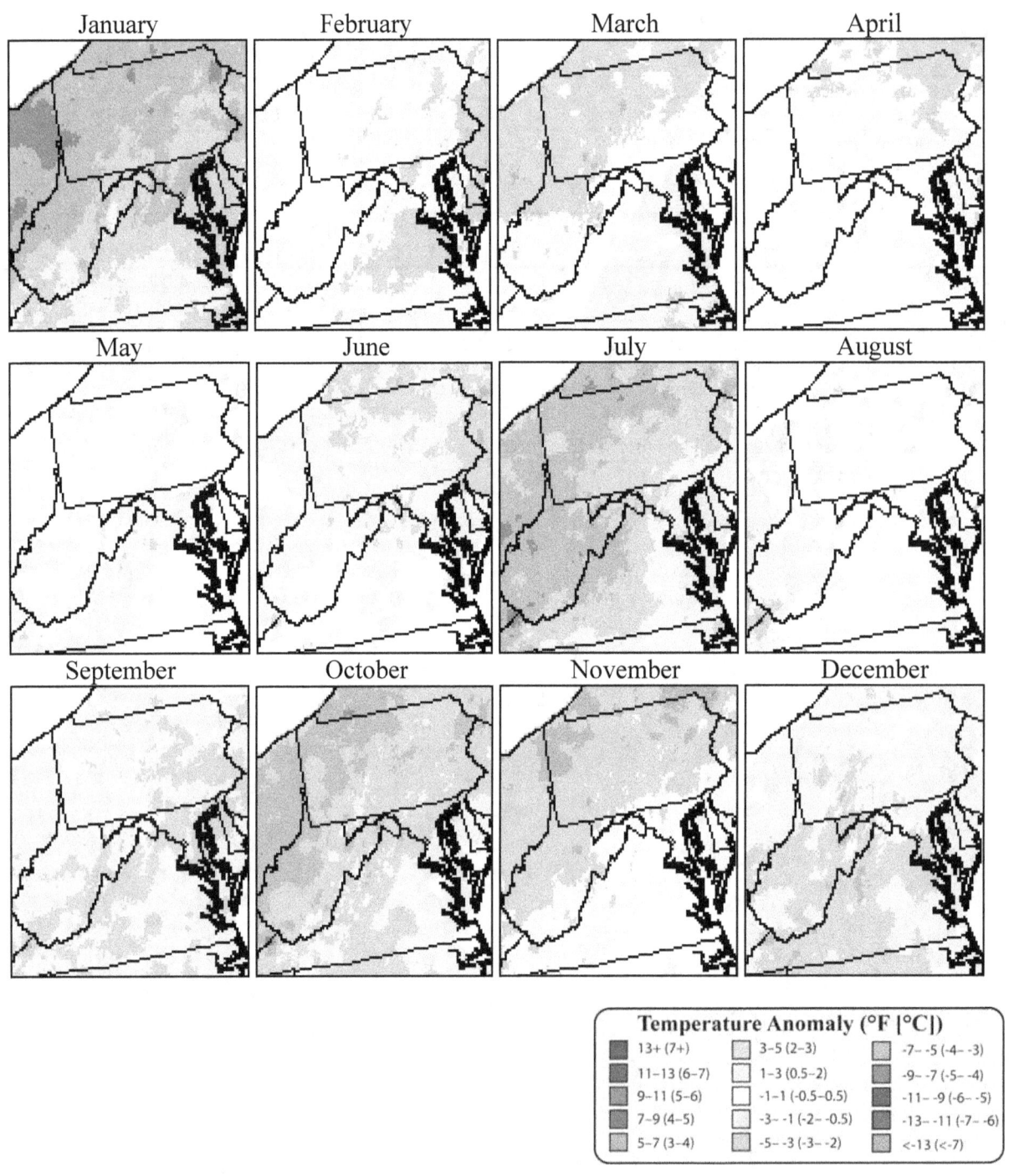

Figure 2. Maps showing departure from average monthly maximum temperature compared to the 30-year normal (1971–2000).

Friendship Hill NHS and Fort Necessity NB
Departure from Average Monthly Minimum Temperature
2009 vs. 1971–2000

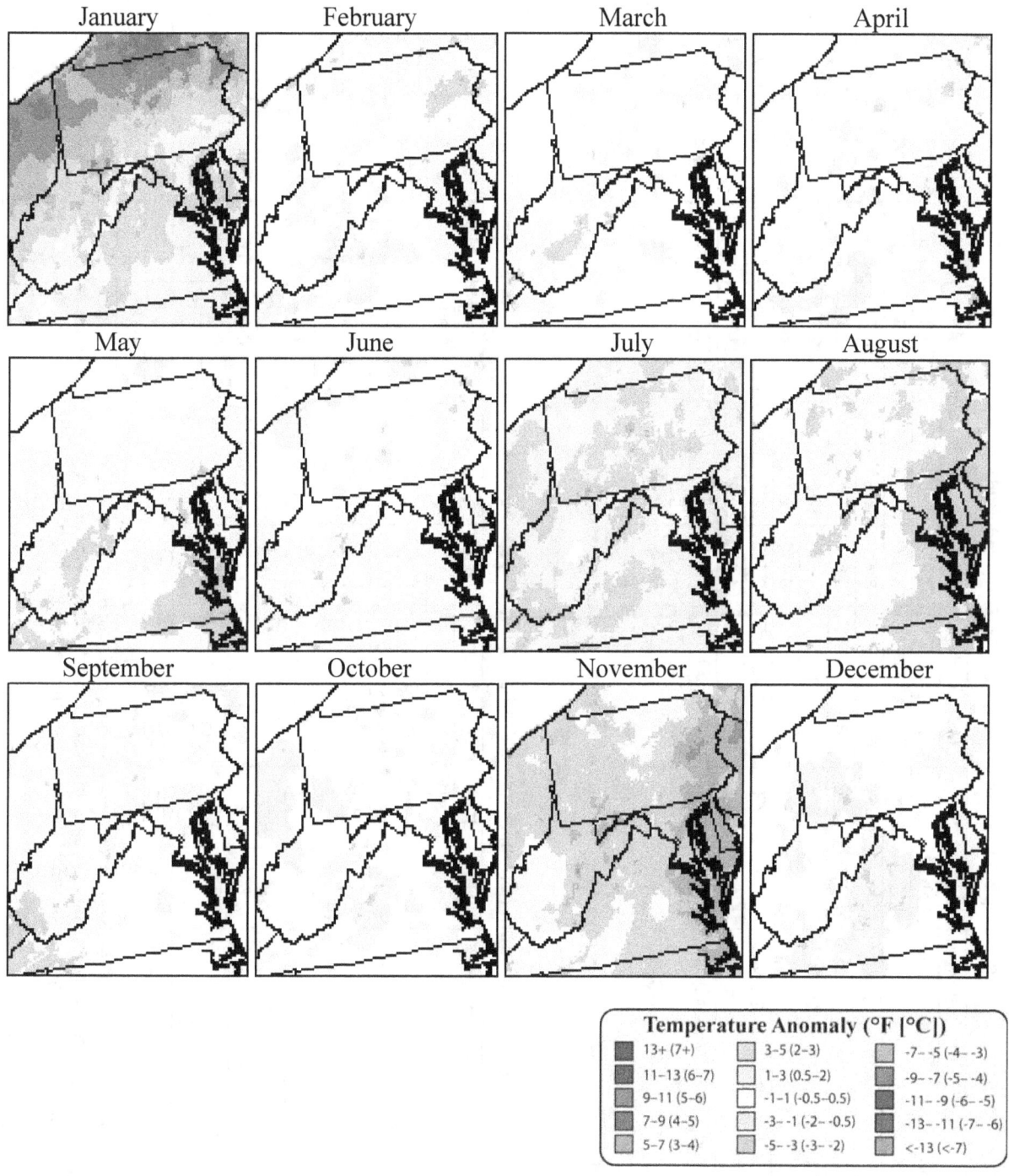

Figure 3. Maps showing departure from average monthly minimum temperature compared to the 30-year normal (1971–2000).

Table 3. Summary of monthly average temperatures for 2009 for the selected stations.

Station name	Station	Jan	Feb	Mar	Apr	May	Jun	Jul	Aug	Sep	Oct	Nov	Dec	Annual
Morgantown Airport, WV	KMGW	26.9°F	34.2°F	44.8°F	52.9°F	62.3°F	68.8°F	70.3°F	74.3°F	67.0°F	54.0°F	50.2°F	34.2°F	53.3°F
		-2.8°C	1.2°C	7.1°C	11.6°C	16.8°C	20.4°C	21.3°C	23.5°C	19.5°C	12.2°C	10.1°C	1.2°C	13.2°C
Chalk Hill, PA	CHKP1	19.5°F	26.4°F	37.0°F	46.2°F	56.4°F	61.8°F	62.5°F	66.4°F	59.2°F	45.7°F	43.5°F	26.1°F	45.9°F
		-7.0°C	-3.1°C	2.8°C	7.9°C	13.6°C	16.6°C	17°C	19.1°C	15.1°C	7.6°C	6.4°C	-3.3°C	11.8°C
Uniontown, PA	UNTP1	25.4°F	32.6°F	42.1°F	50.9°F	61.5°F	67.5°F	68.5°F	72.3°F	65.4°F	50.6°F	48.9°F	31.4°F	51.4°F
		-3.7°C	0.3°C	5.6°C	10.5°C	16.4°C	19.7°C	20.3°C	22.4°C	18.6°C	10.3°C	9.4°C	-0.3°C	13.4°C
Confluence, PA	CONP1	21.6°F	29.7°F	39.0°F	47.5°F	58.7°F	64.8°F	66.1°F	70.2°F	62.0°F	48.1°F	45.6°F	28.9°F	48.5°F
		-5.8°C	-1.3°C	3.9°C	8.6°C	14.8°C	18.2°C	19.0°C	21.2°C	16.6°C	9.0°C	7.5°C	-1.7°C	13.2°C
Morgantown Lock and Dam, WV	MOEW2	25.2°F	31.8°F	42.1°F	50.5°F	61.1°F	67.6°F	68.7°F	72.1°F	64.9°F	51.1°F	47.7°F	32.7°F	51.3°F
		-3.8°C	-0.1°C	5.6°C	10.3°C	16.2°C	19.8°C	20.4°C	22.3°C	18.3°C	10.6°C	8.7°C	0.4°C	13.3°C
Grays Landing, PA	GYLP1	25.0°F	31.8°F	41.3°F	48.9°F	59.9°F	M	67.8°F	71.9°F	64.3°F	50.3°F	47.0°F	30.4°F	49.0°F
		-3.9°C	-0.1°C	5.2°C	9.4°C	15.5°C	M	19.9°C	22.2°C	17.9°C	10.2°C	8.3°C	-0.9°C	13.6°C

M = missing data (Monthly statistics are reported as' M' if greater than 4 days of data are missing).

Table 4. Summary of 2009 departure from normal temperature based on 30-year normal (1971–2000) for the selected stations.

Station name	Station	Jan	Feb	Mar	Apr	May	Jun	Jul	Aug	Sep	Oct	Nov	Dec	Annual
Chalk Hill, PA	CHKP1	-6.6°F	-2.7°F	-0.9°F	-1.9°F	-0.9°F	-3.1°F	-6.1°F	-0.8°F	-1.3°F	-4.3°F	3.5°F	-4.7°F	-2.5°F
		-3.7°C	-1.5°C	-0.5°C	-1.1°C	-0.5°C	-1.7°C	-3.4°C	-0.4°C	-0.7°C	-2.4°C	1.9°C	-2.6°C	-1.4°C
Grays Landing, PA*	GYLP1	-3.9°F	0.4°F	1.5°F	-0.5°F	0.5°F	M	-4.3°F	1.4°F	0.6°F	-1.7°F	4.5°F	-3.3°F	M
		-2.2°C	0.2°C	0.8°C	-0.3°C	0.3°C	M	-2.4°C	0.8°C	0.3°C	-0.9°C	2.5°C	-1.8°C	M
Uniontown, PA	UNTP1	-3.5°F	1.2°F	2.3°F	1.5°F	2.1°F	-0.5°F	-3.6°F	1.8°F	1.7°F	-1.4°F	6.4°F	-2.3°F	0.5°F
		-1.9°C	0.7°C	1.3°C	0.8°C	1.2°C	-0.3°C	-2.0°C	1.0°C	0.9°C	-0.8°C	3.6°C	-1.3°C	0.3°C
Confluence, PA	CONP1	-5.0°F	0.4°F	0.9°F	-0.9°F	0.2°F	-2.4°F	-5.2°F	0.0°F	-1.1°F	-3.2°F	4.8°F	-2.3°F	-1.2°F
		-2.8°C	0.2°C	0.5°C	-0.5°C	0.1°C	-1.3°C	-2.9°C	0.0°C	-0.6°C	-1.8°C	2.7°C	-1.3°C	-0.7°C
Morgantown Lock and Dam, WV	MOEW2	-5.6°F	-1.9°F	0.5°F	-1.8°F	0.2°F	-1.8°F	-4.9°F	0.0°F	-0.9°F	-3.3°F	3.4°F	-2.7°F	-1.6°F
		-3.1°C	-1.1°C	0.3°C	-1.0°C	0.1°C	-1.0°C	-2.7°C	0.0°C	-0.5°C	-1.8°C	1.9°C	-1.5°C	-0.9°C
Morgantown, WV	KMGW	-3.5°F	0.7°F	2.5°F	1.0°F	1.1°F	-0.3°F	-2.9°F	2.4°F	1.7°F	-0.2°F	5.9°F	-0.8°F	0.6°F
		-1.9°C	0.4°C	1.4°C	0.6°C	0.6°C	-0.2°C	-1.6°C	1.3°C	0.9°C	-0.1°C	3.3°C	-0.4°C	0.3°C

M = missing data (Monthly statistics are reported as' M' if greater than 4 days of data are missing).

*Indicates a station's period of record is less than 30 years. In these cases, the departure from normal values were calculated with normals derived from data spanning the length of the station's period of record. Stations with a period of record of less than 5 years were not included in this table.

Table 5. Seasonal temperature and precipitation rankings over 115 years (1 = warmest/wettest year and 115 = coldest/driest year) for Pennsylvania Climate Division 9.

PA Climate Division 9 Rankings "Southwest"	Jan–Feb–Mar WINTER	Apr–May–Jun SPRING	Jul–Aug–Sep SUMMER	Oct–Nov–Dec AUTUMN
Temperature-2009	72	68	104	63
Precipitation-2009	94	31	73	44

Precipitation Summary

Overall, 50.6 in (1,285 mm) of liquid precipitation (rain plus melted snow, ice, sleet, etc.; hereafter precipitation) fell in Chalk Hill, PA (near Fort Necessity NB), and 41.7 in (1,059 mm) in Morgantown Lock and Dam, WV (near Friendship Hill NHS) during the year (Table 6). The longest dry spells of the year occurred between August 31 to September 21 when only three of the 22 days noted measurable rainfall at Chalk Hill (Table 7). Conversely, one of the wetter days in 2009 occurred on October 10 when 1.9 in (49 mm) fell in Chalk Hill (Table 7). There were no influences, either direct or indirect, from tropical storms in this period. Precipitation varied during 2009 at Fort Necessity NB and Friendship Hill NHS with precipitation above normal in five months, below normal in five months, and near normal in two months (Tables 8 and 9); oddly this is the same distribution as in 2008.

The winter season started with a wetter-than-average January with 4.7 in (120 mm [109% of average]) precipitation falling at Chalk Hill (Tables 8 and 9). However, February turned drier, with precipitation ranging from 1.4 in (35mm) at Grays Landing to 3.6 in (91 mm) at Chalk Hill (Table 8). March was quite dry, ranking as the 27th driest in 115 years of record in Pennsylvania Climate Division 9. Due, in part, to a dry February and March, the winter (January, February, and March) ranked as the 21st driest since 1895 (Table 5). Snowfall near Fort Necessity NB was below normal with 74.9 in (190.2 cm) falling in Chalk Hill, which was below the average of 88.7 in (225.3 cm) (Table 6).

April precipitation was slightly below normal with 4.3 in (110 mm) falling on Chalk Hill and 3.7 in (93 mm) falling on Grays Landing (Table 8). May ranked as the 32nd wettest with 9.0 in (229 mm) falling on Grays Landing (Table 8). Positive anomalies persisted in June with the region averaging about 115% of normal (Table 9). Overall, spring of 2009 ranked as the 31st wettest in this climate division (Table 5).

Summer of 2009 was somewhat drier than average (Figure 4). It ranked as the 42nd driest (Table 5). The deficit was caused by a dry July and a very dry September, which was 37th driest since 1895. July had 2.9 in (73 mm) of rain falling in Grays Landing (72% of normal) and September brought a mere 2.0 in (51 mm) (Tables 8 and 9).

The autumn of 2009 turned wet, ranking as the 44th wettest in 115 years in the Southwest Plateau Pennsylvania Climate Division (Table 5). While October and December were moist, November was the driest month of the year (Figure 4). Precipitation ranged from 0.8 in (20.3 mm) at Grays Landing to 1.6 in (40.6 mm) in Chalk Hill during November (Table 8). This was the 8th driest November on record. A moderate dry spell was noted from November 6–18 (Table 7). Rain and snow returned in earnest during December with 4.7 in (119.4 mm) falling on Confluence (Table 8). The number of heavy precipitation days was below normal in 2009; though the number of days with measurable snow and moderate snow were just about average (Table 6).

Table 6. Status of 2009 precipitation indicators compared to the 30-year normal (1971–2000) at the Chalk Hill (CHKP1) and Morgantown Lock and Dam (MOEW2) stations.

Precipitation Indicator	CHKP1 2009	CHKP1 1971–2000	MOEW2 2009	MOEW2 1971–2000
Annual Precipitation	50.6 in 1,285 mm	54.7 in 1,389 mm	41.7 in 1,059 mm	42.1 in 1,069 mm
Autumn (Oct, Nov, Dec) Precipitation	12.3 in 312 mm	12.2 in 310 mm	8.4 in 213 mm	9.7 in 246 mm
Heavy Rain (days with ≥1.0 in (25 mm) rain)	8	11	6	8
Extreme Rain (days with ≥2.0 in (51 mm) rain)	1	1	1	1
Micro-drought (strings of 7+ days without rain)	5	3	7	6
Annual Snowfall	74.9 in 1,903 mm	88.7 in 2253 mm	18.6 in 472 mm	22.6 in 574 mm
Snow (days with ≥0.1 in (0.3 cm) snow)	51	54	23	19
Moderate Snow (days with ≥2.0 in (5.0 cm) snow)	14	17	2	3
Heavy Snow (days with ≥5.0 in (12.7 cm) snow)	4	4	0	1

Table 7. Top five wettest days and top five dry spells (consecutive days with a trace or less of rainfall) during 2009 from stations at Chalk Hill (CHKP1) and Morgantown Lock and Dam (MOEW2).

Wettest Days in 2009	Dry Spells in 2009
Dec. 9: 2.0 in (50 mm)	Jul. 4–17
May 5: 2.0 in (50 mm)	Mar. 2–14
Oct. 10: 1.9 in (49 mm)	Nov. 6–18
Jun. 18: 1.7 in (43 mm)	Sep. 11–21
Jan. 7: 1.3 in (32 mm)	Aug. 31–Sep. 8

Table 8. Summary of 2009 monthly total precipitation for selected stations.

Station name	Station	Jan	Feb	Mar	Apr	May	Jun	Jul	Aug	Sep	Oct	Nov	Dec	Annual
Morgantown Airport, WV	KMGW	2.8 in	1.8 in	1.7 in	3.8 in	6.3 in	4.6 in	3.3 in	3.7 in	2.6 in	3.9 in	1.0 in	3.2 in	38.7 in
		72 mm	46 mm	43 mm	96 mm	161 mm	117 mm	84 mm	94 mm	66 mm	98 mm	25 mm	81 mm	983 mm
Cha k Hill, PA	CHKP1	4.7 in	3.6 in	2.4 in	4.3 in	7.1 in	4.9 in	3.2 in	4.7 in	3.4 in	6.1 in	1.6 in	4.6 in	50.6 in
		120 mm	91 mm	60 mm	110 mm	181 mm	125 mm	82 mm	119 mm	86 mm	155 mm	40 mm	117 mm	1,285 mm
Uniontown, PA	UNTP1	3.4 in	1.7 in	2.0 in	3.0 in	6.0 in	2.8 in	3.3 in	3.1 in	2.2 in	4.5 in	1.2 in	3.3 in	36.5 in
		87 mm	44 mm	50 mm	76 mm	153 mm	70 mm	85 mm	79 mm	55 mm	134 mm	30 mm	84 mm	927 mm
Confluence, PA	CONP1	3.8 in	2.0 in	1.2 in	3.6 in	5.6 in	7.0 in	3.7 in	3.5 in	2.0 in	5.9 in	1.2 in	4.7 in	44.3 in
		98 mm	50 mm	30 mm	90 mm	143 mm	178 mm	95 mm	89 mm	51 mm	150 mm	31 mm	119 mm	1,125 mm
Morgantown Lock and Dam, WV	MOEW2	4.0 in	2.0 in	1.7 in	4.1 in	7.1 in	4.6 in	2.9 in	4.4 in	2.6 in	3.8 in	0.9 in	3.7 in	41.7 in
		101 mm	50 mm	44 mm	105 mm	181 mm	117 mm	73 mm	111 mm	65 mm	95 mm	23 mm	95 mm	1,059 mm
Grays Landing, PA	GYLP1	3.1 in	1.4 in	2.0 in	3.7 in	9.0 in	M	2.9 in	3.7 in	2.0 in	4.6 in	0.8 in	3.7 in	M
		79 mm	35 mm	50 mm	93 mm	228 mm	M	73 mm	95 mm	51 mm	116 mm	20 mm	93 mm	M

M = missing data (Monthly statistics are reported as' M' if greater than 4 days of data are missing).

Table 9. Summary of 2009 percent of normal precipitation based on 30-year normal (1971–2000) for selected stations.

Station name	Station	Jan	Feb	Mar	Apr	May	Jun	Jul	Aug	Sep	Oct	Nov	Dec	Annual
Morgantown Airport, WV	KMGW	98	67	46	107	152	112	78	92	74	136	30	103	91
Chalk Hill, PA	CHKP1	109	95	50	86	136	103	58	110	75	167	37	113	95
Uniontown, PA	UNTP1	115	62	54	80	138	64	72	79	60	155	34	107	85
Confluence, PA	CONP1	109	67	31	90	126	175	78	94	50	197	33	134	98
Morgantown Lock and Dam, WV	MOEW2	122	68	45	112	163	114	68	110	76	131	25	115	96
Grays Landing, PA	GYLP1	97	59	53	100	209	M	72	103	70	187	24	131	M

M = missing data (Monthly statistics are reported as 'M' if greater than 4 days of data are missing).

*Indicates a station's period of record is less than 30 years. In these cases, the departure from normal values was calculated with normals derived from data spanning the length of the station's period of record. Stations with a period of record of less than 5 years were not included in this table.

Friendship Hill NHS and Fort Necessity NB
Percent of Average Monthly Precipitation
2009 vs. 1971–2000

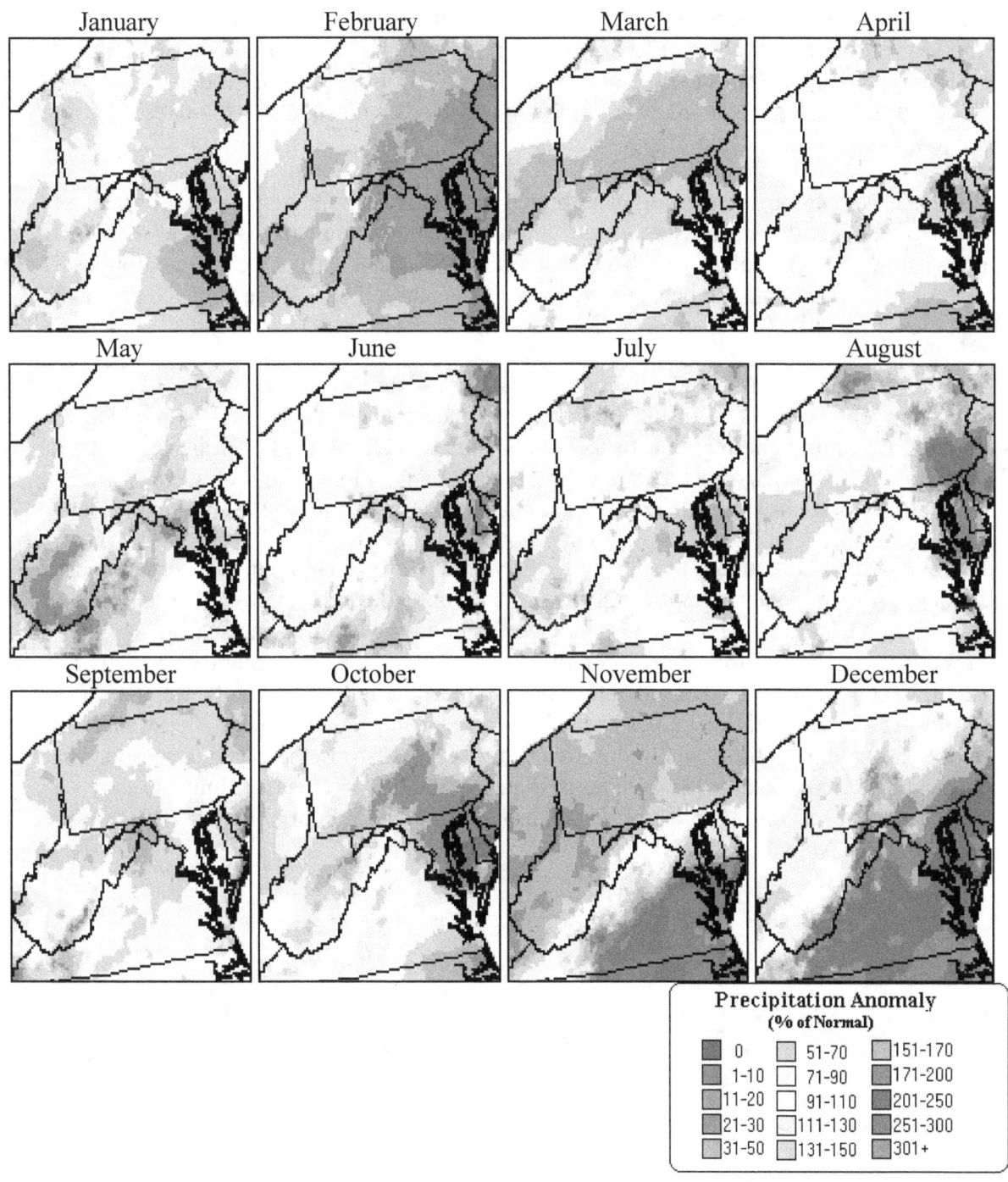

Figure 4. Maps showing percent of average monthly precipitation compared to the 30-year normal (1971–2000).

Drought Status

There are a number of drought indices used to estimate the severity of drought in an area using algorithms that incorporate recent temperatures, rainfall, soil moisture, and other information (http://www.drought.gov). The main indices we report are the Palmer Drought Severity Index (PDSI) and the United States Drought Monitor (DM) – Drought Intensity Index. While both indices provides excellent summary information on broad-scale conditions, local conditions (such as at the park scale) may vary.

The PDSI is a soil moisture algorithm calibrated for relatively homogeneous regions and is calculated on a monthly basis using precipitation and temperature data, as well as the water content of the soil. The values vary between extremely moist (>4.0) and extreme drought (<-4.0) with "normal" values ranging between -1.9 and 1.9. Monthly PDSI values for Pennsylvania Climate Division 9 in 2009 are shown in Figure 5.

The DM – Drought Intensity Index is a synthesis of multiple indices (including the PDSI) and impacts and represents a consensus of federal and academic scientists. The DM produces a summary map of drought intensity for the nation and all states each week. It is on a scale ranging from abnormally dry (D0) to exceptional drought (D4). Mid-month (i.e., the second or third week) values for Pennsylvania (Figure 6) and the Northeast (Figure 7) are shown for 2009.

According to the PDSI, after a moist start to the year in Climate Division 9, a very dry spring led the drought severity index to approach "moderate drought" level by late April (Figure 5) but it remained in the "normal" range. Near average rainfall during the growing season kept the PDSI values positive ("moist") from May through August; however, a dry September and an exceptionally dry November caused values to drop to negative ("dry") levels. Regular rain and snow during December raised values back above normal (0). Calendar year 2009 was most similar to 2007, though the dry period in that year occurred during the growing season. The DM – Drought Severity Index for Pennsylvania (Figure 6) and the Northeast (Figure 7) shows a similar pattern for the growing season (May through October); abnormally dry (D0) only during the beginning of May.

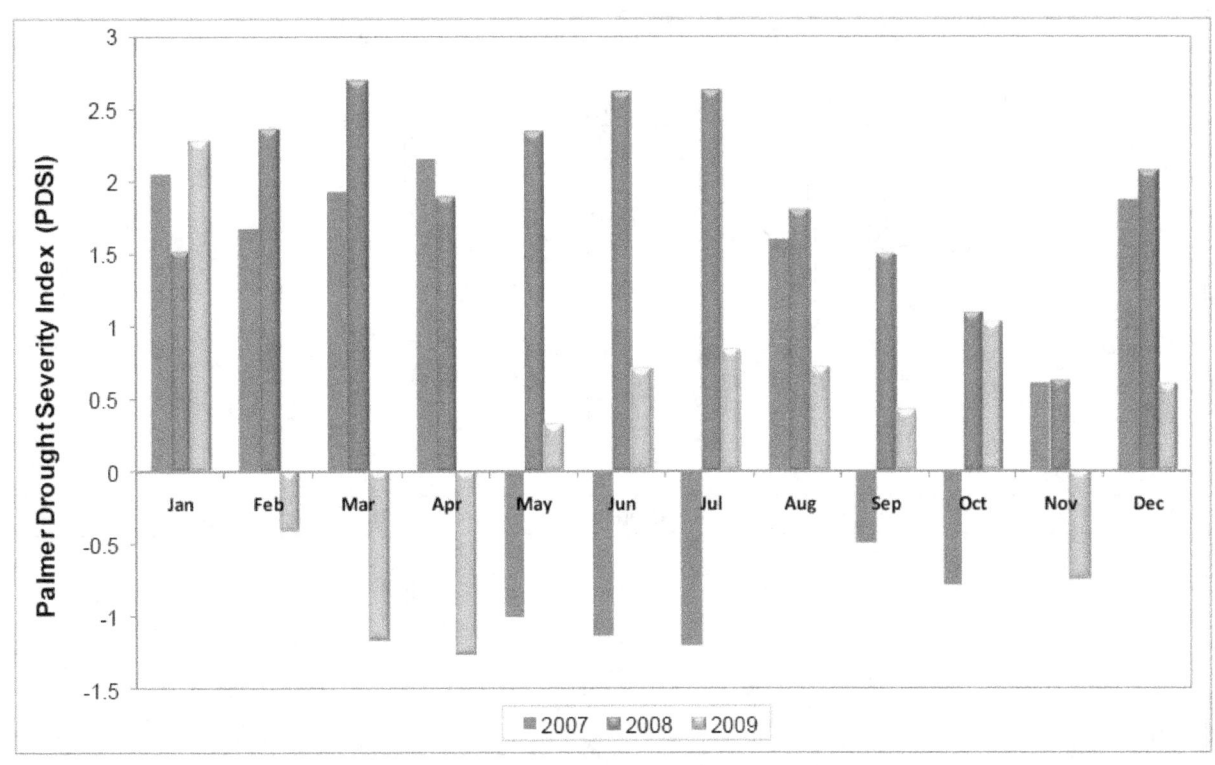

Figure 5. Monthly Palmer Drought Severity Index (PDSI) values for Pennsylvania Climate Division 9, 2007–2009.

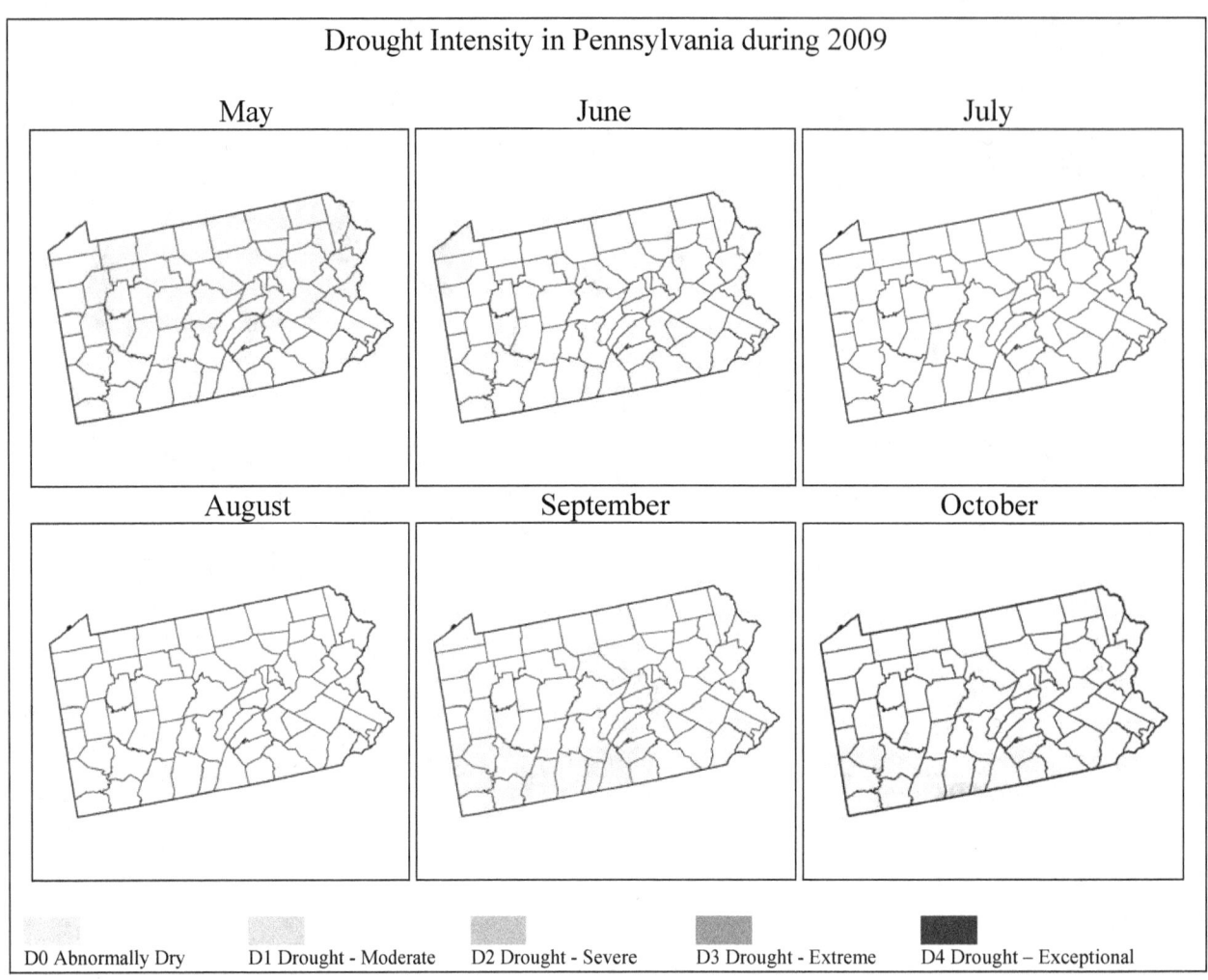

Figure 6. Mid-month values of the Drought Monitor – Drought Intensity Index for Pennsylvania in 2009.

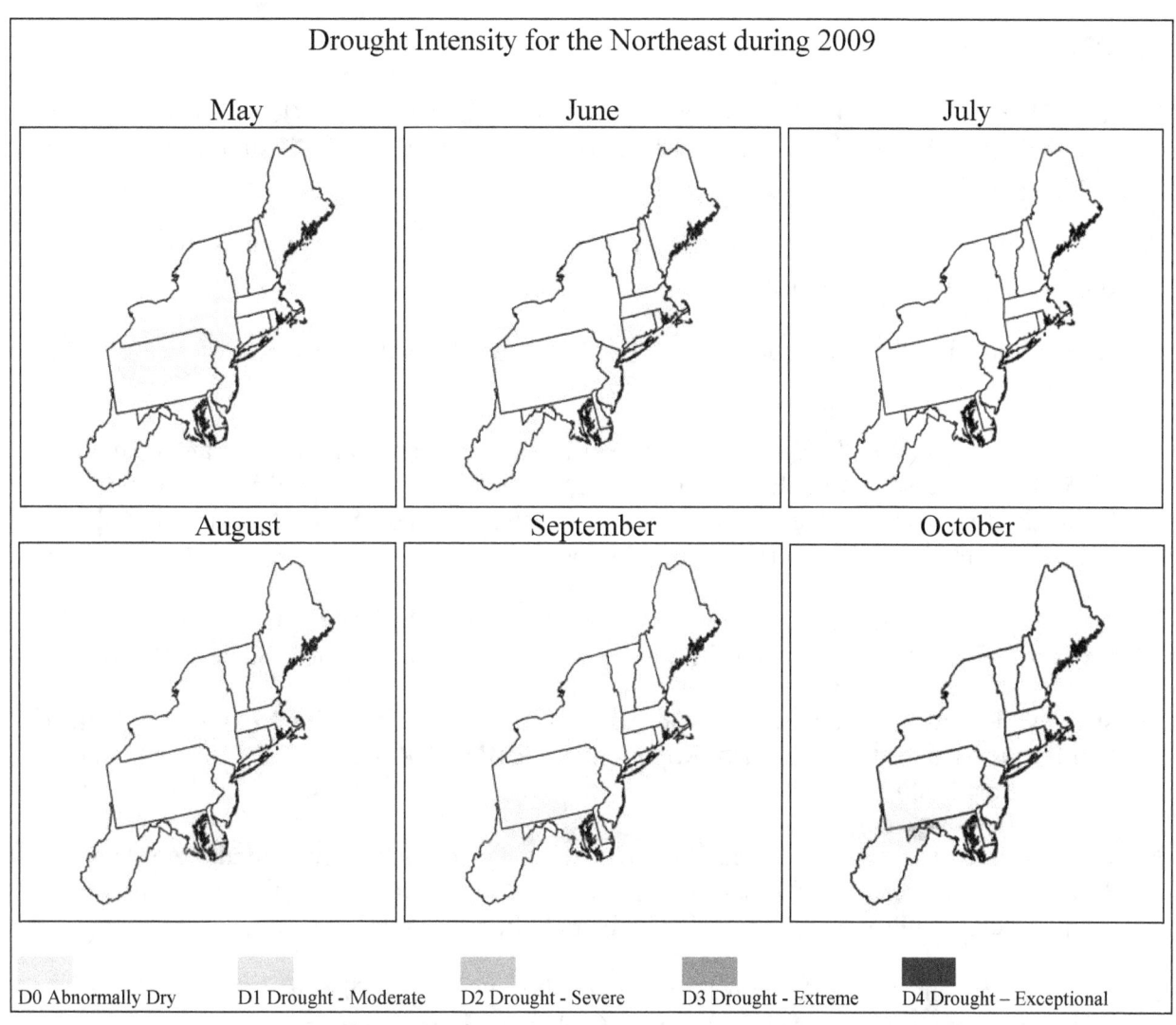

Figure 7. Mid-month values of the Drought Monitor – Drought Intensity Index for the Northeast in 2009.

References

Bureau of Land Management. 1997. Remote Automatic Weather Station (RAWS) and Remote Environmental Monitoring Systems (REMS) standards. RAWS/REMS Support Facility, Boise, ID.

Daly, C., W. P. Gibson, G. H. Taylor, G. L. Johnson, and P. Pasteris. 2002. A knowledge-based approach to the statistical mapping of climate. Climate Research 22:99–113.

Gelber, B. 2002. The Pennsylvania Weather Book. Rutgers University Press. New Brunswick, NJ.

Knight, P., T. Wisniewski, C. Bahrmann, and S. Miller. In preparation. Weather and Climate Monitoring Protocol for the Eastern Rivers and Mountains Network and Mid-Atlantic Network of the National Park Service. Natural Resource Report Series NPS/ERMN/NRR—2010/XXX. National Park Service, Fort Collins, CO.

Kocin, P. J., and L. W. Uccellini. 2004. Northeast Snowstorms Volume 1: Overview. Meteorological Monographs. Vol 32. No 54. American Meteorological Society. Boston, MA.

Marshall, M. R., and N. B. Piekielek. 2007. Eastern Rivers and Mountains Network Ecological Monitoring Plan. Natural Resource Report NPS/ERMN/NRR—2007/017. National Park Service. Fort Collins, CO.

National Assessment Synthesis Team. 2001. Climate Change Impacts on United States: The Potential Consequences of Climate Variability and Change, Report for the U.S. Global Change Research Program. Cambridge University Press, Cambridge, UK.

National Oceanic and Atmospheric Administration (NOAA). 2008. National Climatic Data Center. Climate of 2008 – Annual Review, Global and U.S. Summary. http://lwf.ncdc.noaa.gov/oa/climate/research/2008/ann/us-summary.html.

The Department of the Interior protects and manages the nation's natural resources and cultural heritage; provides scientific and other information about those resources; and honors its special responsibilities to American Indians, Alaska Natives, and affiliated Island Communities.

NPS 336/105525, 476/105525, September 010

National Park Service
U.S. Department of the Interior

Natural Resource Program Center
1201 Oakridge Drive, Suite 150
Fort Collins, CO 80525

http://www.nature.nps.gov

EXPERIENCE YOUR AMERICA ™